STRAWBERRIES

Jo Morris Dixon is the author of two poetry pamphlets: I *told you everything* (Verve Poetry Press: 2021) and *Strawberries* (Broken Sleep Books: 2025). She has had individual poems appear in: *Oxford Poetry, Ambit, The Poetry Review, bath magg,* and *fourteen poems*. In addition, they have had poems anthologized in *100 Queer Poems* (Vintage Press: 2022), *He She They Us* (Pan Macmillan: 2024) and *You're Never Too Much: poems for every emotion* (Pan Macmillan: 2025).

Also by Jo Morris Dixon

I told you everything   (Verve Poetry Press, 2021)

PRAISE for *Strawberries*

Tender and deliciously complex, *Strawberries* is a pamphlet that feels both deeply personal and remarkably relatable. Dixon weaves together memories, emotions and reflections in such a vulnerable and poignant way There is a unique voice here, one with such emotional honesty, inviting you to explore these moments of joy, loss and devastation. I was truly, profoundly moved.

— Luís Costa

Jo Morris Dixon writes with a steady eye and an open heart. The body is at the centre of these intimate poems - queer, loving, grieving - and the physical propels the texts in their explorations of vulnerability and resilience. Courageous, both in form and content, *Strawberries* is a pamphlet which reminds us that "being alive we have to try harder."

— Ella Duffy

This is such a vulnerable and authentic collection of poems from a fresh queer voice. I particularly love the rich use of details and imagery that creates a vibrant, candid, and complex world on the page. A collection worth rereading and contemplating.

— Golnoosh Nour

Jo Morris Dixon's *Strawberries* is a searing reflection of our tempestuous times – an unflinching exploration of the human condition that resonates deeply with the anxieties of our present moment.

— Kostya Tsolakis

CONTENTS

for B.H. & her rooms: thank you

ISBN: 978-1-917617-27-7

The author has asserted their right to be identified as the author of this Work in accordance with the Copyright, Designs and Patents Act 1988

Cover designed by Aaron Kent

Edited and Typeset by Aaron Kent

Broken Sleep Books Ltd
PO BOX 102
Llandysul
SA44 9BG

Strawberries

Jo Morris Dixon

Broken Sleep Books

I used to believe that if you write things down
you can keep them away from you.
— Emily Berry, *Unexhausted Time*

I don't know whether I ever want you to read this,
but I know that I need to write it.
— Tomasz Jedrowski, *Swimming in the Dark*

The books I'm writing are houses that I build for myself.
— Etel Adnan

PLAYTIME

there were good days / during the holidays / when your
mum made us / vegetarian pasta bakes / with salad from
a plastic packet / which she trusted us / to wash and let us
/ choose any film we wanted / so we watched things / to
make us feel older / than we actually were at ten / and
because I always wore shorts and a t-shirt / you told me I
could play Leonardo Di-Caprio / which made us excited
to try things / like me drawing you / that summer we
learnt / that we had parts like boys / which felt good too /
and that these were too special / to be graffitied on desks

DO YOU REMEMBER WHEN I TRIED TO BE GOOD
after Ocean Vuong

I wore a dress to my aunt's sixtieth birthday party.

It was a bad time.

I wasn't the right person for him.

How could anyone want to live again.

One day the sun will stop burning & I won't

be there to help other people & everything

alive makes me grieve. A fool, I still go to therapy

just to confirm that I care.

It was too dark & I left the house with my dead phone.

I still think about my pet goldfish buried

in Golden Syrup tins. Meaningful things

won't always be happy things.

I came out to my Reverand by email & felt like praying.

On the coach to Yosemite, I watched two people

like me hold hands. I tried to make eye contact

but it was like trying to control a dream

when you're just about to wake up.

I have a drawer in my room just for stones.

My dad is worried that his uncle was a Nazi.

I kept a notebook as a teenager for important information.

Genocides. I know how they happen.

People will do anything to be good.

I fell through ice & breathed in smoke to keep warm

but we don't talk about that.

PERIOD PAD

I was so upset

with my period

I ripped my pad

off and squeezed

it in my fist

because I couldn't

punch it out of me

like the bullies

at school waiting

for me when

no one else did

BEING ALIVE MEANS WE NEED TO TRY HARDER

before the library turned into a swimming pool

for insects after the construction workers brought

it down leaving book-shaped holes left to be filled

with rain I fantasized about you sitting next to me

writing answers to all the questions I didn't know

to ask on rectangular paper too small to hide behind

pale blue to make me move like how I did in water

which made me think of that time I told you dying

would help our planet more than buying a moon-

cup or encouraging people to adopt children instead

of making them I told you dying would make me feel

better about the climate crisis knowing that would

entail no carbon footprint just my body feeding sea

creatures but a robin came up to us on our bench

and you said being alive means we need to try harder

IN MEDIAS RES

that's where you'll see the chairs
one low round table under water
in a jug that's hard to hold next to
my glass that's already full whilst
yours is left empty next to a card-
board box of tissues which look
like waves when there's thunder
look to the right and you will see
where I stand when I'm thinking
about all of my problems instead
of yours don't hurt yourself when
you sit opposite me but tilt your
head backwards a bit or just turn
around and you'll see the ugliest
face in the world how time stops
just when we start to understand
ourselves look up and don't stop
thinking until you remember stars
die too make yourself look away
from the yellow vase without
flowers to the right of my chair
instead let me hold you without
touching look at me when you cry

FREESTYLE

I had a dream which was an actual
nightmare where a man woke up
before me but what was interesting
about it was how he walked out
of my body which was sleeping
and I watched him do everything
I had ever wanted to do like feel
good topless with boxers showing
above his jeans writing poems before
swimming freestyle in speedos so
fast I felt proud of him and I heard
my therapist telling me again how
repetition is important but now
I wanted to tell her how for ages
my breaststroke kick was out of
time and it took ages to correct
which is what happens when you
repeat the wrong things over again

HOPPER'S GAZE

like most things important it took longer to realise
than it should have but looking at Edward Hopper's
paintings of women in rooms before COVID-19
makes me angry at his simplified version of women
reinforcing our sexist roles in the home staring out
of windows instead of painting them
like the men who dominate the art galleries

Room in New York depicts a woman in a dress
sitting on a piano stool in a way which would make
composing her own piece of music impossible
whilst the man in the picture
reads the newspaper in his waistcoat and tie
an outfit which maybe the woman wanted to wear
whilst she danced in one of the few dyke bars

but instead wakes up frustrated and alone
like the woman in *Morning Sun* with her husband
out of the picture and sleeping with whoever
he wants since he controls their finances so she
gazes out of the window her only comfort
the colour blue and an empty bed

ONLINE THERAPY SESSION

Hi

    Hi

      [long pause]

How are you?

        Fine.

          [Therapist moves closer to the screen]

How does it feel

      to feel fine?

[Client pushes laptop away]

STAR SIGN

I thought I knew what the C word was

the word which I found engraved into my desk at school

spraypainted onto the side of trains going nowhere

the word which Chaucer used but we couldn't

but now I know the real C word is cancer

the worst star sign to have

DEATH TOLL ON BBC RADIO 4 AT BREAKFAST TIME

you wanted me to listen to the death toll whilst you ate your bowl of cereal
telling me that it would all get better soon even though my sister was waiting
to hear back about the date for her operation to remove her malignant tumour

which made it sound better than saying it was cancerous when of course
that's what it meant when the Macmillan Cancer Nurse explained on loud-
speaker when talking to my sister about her biopsy at the height of COVID-19

during lockdown in January 2021 and I was back in my childhood bedroom
googling *chondrosarcoma* for the first time wishing that I was a surgeon
instead so I could be of more use than saying to my sister that I would always

be there for her but of course the restrictions meant that it was impossible
to do anything other than speak to her when she woke up from her pain
relief calling up the nurses to ask if they could kindly check on her despite you

saying that we should trust the nurses I wanted to scream or hold up Munch's

famous painting as protest but that would be pretentious so I said defiantly

that I would want someone to call up to check on me which made you spill

your coffee as you turned up the radio again to listen to testimonials from people

crying about not being able to have their cancer operations and spending their last

weeks on planet earth in a hospice with only their phones for comfort as they died

you wanted me to listen to the death toll every time I went into the kitchen telling

me that it would all get better soon even though my sister was only 26

and had been diagnosed with a rare cancer during a pandemic you wanted me

to listen to the death toll you said it was important to know what was happening

as if I didn't know that people were dying every day you told me to smile

IT FEELS LIKE I'M TRAPPED IN A CHEKHOV PLAY

[she sits on an armchair in the living room

the sun is shining in an inconvenient way]

my sister has been diagnosed with bone cancer

[the cat called Lulu is staring through the window

her owner has just put their house on the market]

my sister's tumour has successfully been removed

[she pulls the wooden coffee table closer with both feet

but nearly causes the remote control to fall to the floor]

my sister's tumour might have been growing for years

[she looks up at the light bulb which must be replaced

but she has an irrational fear of being electrocuted]

my sister had surgeons operate on her for six hours

MY OMA'S COUSIN WAS A PSYCHOTHERAPIST WHO KNEW CARL JUNG

for ten weeks we met on the back seat

of my parents' diesel car you kept your

hands to yourself because that's what

you always did even when we met in-

person before therapy moved online

and I had to get my own water or just

sit there thirsty remembering how it

felt to make dinner alone as a child

cutting myself on the sharp edge of

tinned tomatoes to see if my parents

were right when they said it would

hurt and that red was the background

colour for the swastika which my oma

would have seen on flags outside her

home in Amsterdam before her cousin

became friends with Carl Jung a man

who listened to clients like you listened

to me whilst your next-door neighbours'

cocker spaniels barked which made me

remember that I wasn't your only client

and that cancer happens to lots of people

not just my sister who got her diagnosis

in January 2021 which made me worry
that you had cancer too or would get it
soon so I stopped talking about the size
of my sister's tumour and how Johnson's
terrible mistakes meant that my sister
would need to self-isolate for two weeks
keep testing negative before she could
have her operation followed by liquid
morphine how I had nightmares about
the surgeons under the bright lights of
an operating theatre when the pandemic
had shut all theatres across the UK my
sister got the chance to perform un-
conscious and how it gave me the idea
to paint a picture of a tree growing
through the tilled floor of a derelict
swimming pool which I told you about
while I held your face in my hand on
my phone as the days got longer in spite
of everything feeling like it was ending
the same daffodils protested their way
through the soil where I buried my gold-
fish in Golden Syrup tins with a bit of
water in case they needed it in heaven

STRAWBERRIES

my mum's best friend
left strawberries
on our porch
she even left me
an Easter egg once
but I was in the car
going back to London
when she got given a bed
in hospital in spring 2021
they only let her leave
for the hospice
where she had jelly
the colour of cancer
in her lungs lasting
for around a decade
till there were no more
drugs left to save her
I had liked her photo
of her newly decorated
bedroom on Instagram
every picture I painted
always got a heart from

my mum's best friend

so I sent her one of my

online therapy rooms

I told her how I picked

a therapist once who

looked exactly like her

I still have our Facebook

messages of when I sent her

aloe vera photos taken quickly

before I changed my mind

just in case she checked

her phone before she

left for the last time

24 HOUR TESCO

it's too late to remember what I came to Tesco for

but I know it had something to do with the last time we spoke

in your room we were both in facemasks and I was thirsty

which made me tell you the truth for once admitting

that I needed a glass of water more than anything else

to carry on you found a glass you were protecting in a drawer

from COVID-19 and walked out of the door for the first time

leaving me alone in the room

like life beyond therapy where you'll leave the world before me

now in Tesco I walk towards the boxes of tissues and think about

whether you've ever had a client who has walked away

with your tissue box before or asked you where you bought

them from so they could have a souvenir with which to say goodbye

WIGMORE HALL

the man I had always wanted

to be stood on stage

at *Wigmore Hall*

adorning the walls and ceiling

with his chords and scales

I was thirty that day

and had only

just seen Monet's waterlilies

you see, heaven and hell

were two of the first

words written down

SOMEDAY

after Ocean Vuong

Jo, don't be afraid.
You won't be alive forever
even though it feels like it
since you'll never know how
it feels not to live. Don't jump
even though you were
taught to follow your heart.
Memorize your triggers & trace
your tears & it will all make sense.
Jo, are you even listening?
Let yourself be held when you cry.
Even the oldest tree in the park
will fall one day. Touch her
bark & it will make you
want to pray to everyone
you have ever loved. God
can be whoever you want
them to be. The Bible was born
from trees & people like you.
Believe in yourself especially
when you dream. You asked
for a second chance & now
you can paint pictures to
accompany music. Jo. Jo –
I think this might be heaven.

WHEN I GET SAD ABOUT EVERYTHING

when I get sad about everything
like all the people who have left
me to live in this world without
them I think about how repetitive
it gets how the world is always
ending for someone I think
about how maybe my oma
woke up and painted her first
self-portrait which meant she forgot
about our trip to see Hilma Af Klint
instead of just being
dead like my mum's best friend
who had a funeral and I decided
to keep her company and closed
my eyes in bed thinking about how
repetitive it gets when I feel sad
about everything like all the people
I left in the world in order to live

HAMPSTEAD HEATH

I went on a date with someone who wrote on her profile how she was *trauma informed* and then when she said on our date that we could play a game whilst we were walking around Hampstead Heath I said *yes* and she said *guess my favourite book* and I immediately wished I had said *no* but that wouldn't have helped at this point since she said *wait, walk slower, it's a really controversial one* and she had full control of the situation now and she looked so happy and I hated the way she smiled how she was so oblivious as to how much my heart had started to hammer and she said *Lolita* and I couldn't hear her properly anymore it sounded like she was miles away as she declared *Lolita* was beautifully written and that it was love story she obviously didn't care that Lolita was sexually abused and that it was told in the voice of her abuser which was so convincing that some readers might actually think that it was a love story and I felt like I had fallen through ice again *look up* and my voice had gone so small like all the stars which might actually be satellites hanging silent in the sky

PRIDE

i loved it when i was lying on top
of someone i had only met once
& she said *i love being queer, do you?*
& i laughed & i said yeah i guess
& she said *well it means you get to*
lie on top of me & i smiled because
she was smiling & sounding indignant
at the same time i said can i kiss you
& she said *you need to answer me first*
yes, I love being queer & we kissed

IF YOU CALL YOURSELF A POET

you might write down lines which you'll call
fragments & I'll think how I read *The Snow Queen*
& became scared of glass shattering
the possibility of becoming the boy
forgotten in a palace needing to be rescued
you might write down lines which you'll want to tell
your therapist before it all ends & I'll think
how I used to look for synonyms for words like sad
to separate myself from the language I felt
everything in but nothing can articulate feelings
as well as the first words we use when we cry &
I'll think how I used to write down lines to be read
at my funeral & you'll wonder if there is something
like a heaven & what about heaven's heaven

if you call yourself a poet – which you might

NOT EVERYONE WRITES POEMS

my therapist was speaking quietly again
the way she does when she's saying something
more important than usual after six years I know her

it matters that she hasn't told me the name
of her cat even though I want her to I've worked
out that she has a partner (probably) who I think
is a therapist too and they live near the Overground
because she didn't know where Queen's Park was but she knew
Kensal Rise and when I said I was moving close to Victoria Park
she immediately said Hackney and the only reason I know
about her cat is because of the pandemic when I would stare
at her office door behind her and I must have mentioned
the elaborate locking system so she told me it was to stop
her cat from coming in but I think she also wanted me
to know that she loves cats too like how I know her favourite
colour must be every kind blue or maybe it's actually
red but that would make me feel like she's dangerous or the one
in danger my therapist was speaking quietly again
the way I imagine she did when she was being told
off as a child it will always make me sad how I'm not
helping her and that sometimes I might even make her
feel worse I know her well now without her telling me
much I understand that she thinks my poems matter

ACKNOWLEDGEMENTS

First and foremost, thank *you* for reading my work.

"Do you remember when I tried to be good" on page 14 is after Ocean Vuong's poem "Theology" published in *The New Yorker* (May 13, 2024)

"Someday" on page 31 is after Ocean Vuong's poem "Someday I'll Love Ocean Vuong" published in *Night Sky With Exit Wounds*.

Am very grateful that the following poems in this pamphlet appear elsewhere:

'Playtime': *He, She, They, Us: An Anthology of Queer Poems* (Macmillan: 2024). '24 Hour Tesco': *You're Never Too Much: poems for every emotion* (Macmillan: 2025). 'freestyle': *fourteen poems, Issue 13*

Thank you to Verve Poetry Press for publishing my debut pamphlet *I told you everything*.

Thank you to Broken Sleep Books for publishing this one.

Thank you to all the libraries and bookshops which hold my work.

Finally, thank you everyone who has helped me along the way. Special thanks to my partner, A, for making me laugh.

LAY OUT YOUR UNREST